VIRGINIA TEST PREP

Writing Workbook

SOL Writing

Grade 4

ISBN 978-1482353501

CONTENTS

INTRODUCTION
For Parents, Teachers, and Tutors

Test Preparation

The SOL Writing test taken by grade 5 students is made up of two parts. In the first part, students answer questions that require planning, composing, editing, or revising a passage. Section 1 of this book will give students practice answering these types of questions. In the second part of the SOL Writing test, students write a story or essay based on a writing prompt. Section 3 of this book will prepare students for this part of the test. Section 2 of this book will develop the specific writing and language skills that students need to perform well on both parts of the SOL Writing test.

In addition, around 25% of the questions on the grade 4 SOL Reading test are word analysis and vocabulary questions. Students can greatly improve their overall score on the test by focusing on improving these skills. Section 2 of this book will develop these essential skills.

Section 1: Revising and Editing Quizzes

Section 1 of this book focuses on editing and revising. It contains 4 sets of 5 passages. Each passage is followed by a question set. These question sets are similar to those on the SOL Writing test, but shorter, and cover the same skills. By completing this section of the book, students will develop the writing skills they need to perform well on the state test, become familiar with the question types on the state test, and gain experience completing revising and editing tasks. Students will then be ready for the SOL Writing test.

Section 2: Language, Vocabulary, and Grammar Quizzes

Section 2 of this book contains individual quizzes focused on each of the writing and language skills that students need. By focusing on each skill individually, students will gain a full understanding of the skill. This will help students perform well on the SOL Writing test and the SOL Reading test.

Section 3: Guided Writing Tasks

Part 3 of this book provides guided practice for the writing tasks that students will encounter on the SOL Writing test. Students will have practice planning and writing stories, personal narratives, and essays. The hints provided with the writing tasks will ensure that students score well when completing writing tasks.

Section 1
Revising and Editing Quizzes

Revising and Editing Quizzes

Set 1

Instructions

Read each passage. Each passage is followed by questions.

For each multiple-choice question, read the question carefully. Then select the best answer. Fill in the circle for the correct answer.

For other types of questions, follow the instructions given.

Building Your Vocabulary

As you read the passages, list any words you do not understand below. Use a dictionary to look up the meaning of the word. Write the meaning of the word below.

Word: _____

Meaning: _____

_____

Word: _____

Meaning: _____

_____

Word: _____

Meaning: _____

_____

Word: _____

Meaning: _____

_____

Word: _____

Meaning: _____

_____

Quiz 1

Read the passage below. Then answer the questions that follow it.

Robot Boy

I'm not a real robot. It's very fun to pretend. My father and I painted a box with silver paint. I glued on bottle tops for buttons. Then my father cut out too holes for my arms. Finally, my father made a large hole to put my head through. I put the box on over my clothes, and I looked just like a real robot.

I enjoy wearing my robot suit outside, in my room, and on the swing. I even weared my robot suit while eating dinner last night. It was hard to get the food in my mouth because I couldn't move my arms easily. I've decided I won't wear my robot suit to dinner anymore.

1   In the passage, the author uses contractions. A contraction is a shortened form of two words. Write the long form of each of the contractions below. The first one has been completed for you.

I'm   _____ I am _____

it's   _____

couldn't   _____

I've   _____

won't   _____

2   Which word rhymes with *suit*?

   Ⓐ   mate

   Ⓑ   wait

   Ⓒ   hoot

   Ⓓ   truth

3   What is the best way to combine the first two sentences?

   Ⓐ   I'm not a real robot, and it's very fun to pretend.

   Ⓑ   I'm not a real robot, for it's very fun to pretend.

   Ⓒ   I'm not a real robot, nor it's very fun to pretend.

   Ⓓ   I'm not a real robot, but it's very fun to pretend.

4   Which word should replace *weared* in the sentence below?

   I even weared my robot suit while eating dinner last night.

   Ⓐ   wear

   Ⓑ   wore

   Ⓒ   wored

   Ⓓ   wearing

5   Which change should be made in the sentence below?

   Then my father cut out too holes for my arms.

   Ⓐ   Change *then* to *than*

   Ⓑ   Change *too* to *two*

   Ⓒ   Change *my* to *mine*

   Ⓓ   Change *arms* to *arm's*

Quiz 2

Read the passage below. Then answer the questions that follow it.

Presidents

In 1789, George Washington became the first president of the United States of America. It is less known that John Adams was the vice president.

John Adams went on to become the second president in 1797. Thomas Jefferson was its vice president.

When John Adams was not any longer president in 1801, Thomas Jefferson became the third president of the United States of America.

George Washington was America's first president. He became president on April 30 1789. He stayed in the role until early 1797.

1   In the word *known*, the letter *k* is silent. For each word below, circle the silent letter in the word. Then write two more words that have the same silent letter.

lamb   _____   _____

ghost   _____   _____

knife   _____   _____

wrong   _____   _____

2   What is the correct way to punctuate the date below?

    Ⓐ   April, 30 1789

    Ⓑ   April 30, 1789

    Ⓒ   April, 30, 1789

    Ⓓ   April 30 1789

3   Which is the best way to rewrite the first part of the sentence below?

When John Adams was not any longer president in 1801, Thomas Jefferson became the third president of the United States of America.

    Ⓐ   When John Adams was not longer president in 1801,

    Ⓑ   When John Adams was no more president in 1801,

    Ⓒ   When John Adams was not anymore president in 1801,

    Ⓓ   When John Adams was no longer president in 1801,

4   Which word should replace *its* in the second sentence below?

John Adams went on to become the second president in 1797. Thomas Jefferson was its vice president.

    Ⓐ   her

    Ⓑ   his

    Ⓒ   him

    Ⓓ   them

Quiz 3

Read the passage below. Then answer the questions that follow it.

Neil Armstrong

Neil Armstrong was the ferst man to Walk on the Moon. He did this in 1969 when he was 38 years old. The American space mission he went on was called Apollo 11. It was during this mission that he said the very well known sentence, "One small step for man, one giant leap for mankind."

He has since been in newspapers. He has since been in magazines. He has been on television, and movies have been made about him. He has even been put onto postage stamps. He worked hard and done something great. He is a great role model for people everywhere.

1   Which change should be made in the sentence below?

He worked hard and done something great.

    Ⓐ   Change *worked* to *working*

    Ⓑ   Change *done* to *did*

    Ⓒ   Change *great* to *grate*

    Ⓓ   There is no change needed.

2   What is the best way to combine the sentences below?

He has since been in newspapers. He has since been in magazines.

Ⓐ   He has since been in newspapers, magazines.

Ⓑ   He has since been in newspapers and magazines.

Ⓒ   He has since been in newspapers and been in magazines.

Ⓓ   He has since been in newspapers, magazines too.

3   Which word in the passage should NOT start with a capital letter?

Ⓐ   Armstrong

Ⓑ   Walk

Ⓒ   American

Ⓓ   Apollo

4   Which word in the passage is spelled incorrectly?

Ⓐ   ferst

Ⓑ   space

Ⓒ   leap

Ⓓ   movies

5   Which word means the opposite of *giant*?

Ⓐ   great

Ⓑ   huge

Ⓒ   brave

Ⓓ   tiny

Quiz 4

Read the passage below. Then answer the questions that follow it.

Stingrays

Stingrays live in the sea. They are related to sharks, but they look very diffrent. They have a long flat body. They have large flat fins. Each fin looks a bit like a giant wing. They are named for the stinger on their tail. The stingers are pointy and sharp. They contain venom or poison.

Stingrays can hide under a thin layer of sand. Because of this, some people have stepped on a stingray and be stung. However, this is not common. In places where people know there are stingrays, they throw small stones into the water before walking through.

1   The passage describe how stingrays have a "long flat body." The words *long* and *flat* are adjectives, or describing words. Complete each sentence below by adding the adjectives used to describe each object.

A stingray's fins are _____ and _____.

Each fin looks a bit like a wing that is _____.

The stingray's stingers are _____ and _____.

Stingray's hide under a layer of sand that is _____.

2   What is the correct way to spell the word *diffrent*?

    Ⓐ   difrent

    Ⓑ   diferent

    Ⓒ   different

    Ⓓ   diffarent

3   Which two words from the passage rhyme?

    Ⓐ   thin, fin

    Ⓑ   look, long

    Ⓒ   stung, stones

    Ⓓ   know, through

4   Which change should be made in the sentence below?

Because of this, some people have stepped on a stingray and be stung.

    Ⓐ   Delete the comma

    Ⓑ   Change *stepped* to *stepping*

    Ⓒ   Change *be* to *been*

    Ⓓ   Change *stung* to *stinged*

5   Which word could replace the words "not common"?

    Ⓐ   commoner

    Ⓑ   commonest

    Ⓒ   uncommon

    Ⓓ   commonly

Quiz 5

Read the passage below. Then answer the questions that follow it.

The Missing Button

James was very upset. When Sarah asked him what was wrong, he told her that he had lost a button from his favorite green coat.

Sarah helped James look for the missing button. They looked around the classroom first. They found a button. It was red. The button that James losed was black. James was glad he had a friend to help him search. They finally found the button under the teachers desk.

1   A compound word is a word made by adding together two different words. The word *classroom* is a compound word made up of the words *class* and *room*. For each compound word below, write three more compounds words that end with the same end word.

classroom

_____room   _____room   _____room

baseball

_____ball   _____ball   _____ball

daytime

_____time   _____time   _____time

2   Which is the best way to combine the sentences below?

They found a button. It was red.

Ⓐ   They found a button, it was red.

Ⓑ   They found a button, so it was red.

Ⓒ   They found a button, but it was red.

Ⓓ   They found a button, then it was red.

3   Which word should replace *losed* in the sentence below?

The button that James losed was black.

Ⓐ   lose

Ⓑ   losing

Ⓒ   lost

Ⓓ   losted

4   Which change should be made in the sentence below?

They finally found the button under the teachers desk.

Ⓐ   Change *they* to *them*

Ⓑ   Change *finally* to *final*

Ⓒ   Change *under* to *undder*

Ⓓ   Change *teachers* to *teacher's*

Revising and Editing Quizzes

Set 2

Instructions

Read each passage. Each passage is followed by questions.

For each multiple-choice question, read the question carefully. Then select the best answer. Fill in the circle for the correct answer.

For other types of questions, follow the instructions given.

Building Your Vocabulary

As you read the passages, list any words you do not understand below. Use a dictionary to look up the meaning of the word. Write the meaning of the word below.

Word: _____

Meaning: _____

_____

Word: _____

Meaning: _____

_____

Word: _____

Meaning: _____

_____

Word: _____

Meaning: _____

_____

Word: _____

Meaning: _____

_____

Quiz 6

Read the passage below. Then answer the questions that follow it.

A Special Day

Dear Diary,

Today, I gone with my friends to get a library card. I had not ever had a library card before. The librarian asked me to sit in a special seat. Then she took my picture. She printed out a card with my name and my photo on it. Then she used a strange machine to cover the card in plastic. She told me how I could use the card to borrow up to four books.

I am so excited to borrow my first book! I want to find a book that has a superhero in it. There is a lot of books, so I am hopeful that I will be able to find one.

Brin

1   Read this sentence from the passage.

I am so excited to borrow my first book!

The author ends this sentence with an exclamation mark. Explain whether this is a suitable punctuation mark to use for the sentence.

_____

_____

_____

_____

2   Which word should replace the word *gone* in the first sentence?

    Ⓐ   go

    Ⓑ   going

    Ⓒ   went

    Ⓓ   done

3   Which word could replace the words "not ever" in the second sentence without changing the meaning of the sentence?

    Ⓐ   neither

    Ⓑ   never

    Ⓒ   always

    Ⓓ   almost

4   What is the correct way to write the first part of the last sentence?

    Ⓐ   There is a lot of book,

    Ⓑ   There is a lots of books,

    Ⓒ   There are a lot of book,

    Ⓓ   There are a lot of books,

5   Which word from the passage has the same start sound as *photo*?

    Ⓐ   gone

    Ⓑ   picture

    Ⓒ   borrow

    Ⓓ   find

Quiz 7

Read the passage below. Then answer the questions that follow it.

Soil

 Soil is necessary to grow most plants. It contains the materials that a plant needs to grow. This includes the water that plants need. Some places, such as deserts, may have soil that does not contain everything that a plant needs. This means that plants are not as likeness to live there.

Good soil usually feels moist, not soaking wet. It is commonly a dark brown color. This is due to all of the animals and plants living in it. A lot of food that people eat comes from plants. The plants keep the soil moving. The animals also add food to the soil.

1   The word *desert* is often misspelled *dessert*. Circle the correct spelling of the commonly misspelled word in each sentence below.

The ferry could hold about one hundred peeple / people.

The kitten was very little / littel.

I have a brother and a sister / sisster.

I am looking for my father and muther / mother.

The park is full of happy chilldren / children.

This book is my favorite / favrite.

2   Which word should replace the word *likeness* in the sentence below?

This means that plants are not as likeness to live there.

Ⓐ   liked

Ⓑ   liking

Ⓒ   likely

Ⓓ   likable

3   What is the best way to rewrite the first sentence of the second paragraph?

Ⓐ   Good soil usually feels moist, so not soaking wet.

Ⓑ   Good soil usually feels moist, and not soaking wet.

Ⓒ   Good soil usually feels moist, nor soaking wet.

Ⓓ   Good soil usually feels moist, but not soaking wet.

4   Which sentence does NOT belong in the passage?

Ⓐ   *Soil is necessary to grow most plants.*

Ⓑ   *It contains the materials that a plant needs to grow.*

Ⓒ   *It is commonly a dark brown color.*

Ⓓ   *A lot of food that people eat comes from plants.*

5   Which word has the same meaning as *necessary*?

Ⓐ   needed

Ⓑ   nice

Ⓒ   likely

Ⓓ   useful

Quiz 8

Read the passage below. Then answer the questions that follow it.

My Duck Family

I am a duck. I go by the name of Frankie. I live in a pond. The pond is in a park. There are many other ducks. It gets very crowded sometimes.

I have three ducklings named Fuzzy, Feathers, and Fergie. We enjoy swimming around the pond. We love eating bread that the kind humans throw to us. Bread tastes very good. Catching the bread first is a fun game to play with my duck family! We often have to fight other ducks for it as well. It can be hard to get the bread, but it's worth it.

©Jan Mehlich

1   The names of the ducks all start with *f*. Place the names of the ducks in alphabetical order.

Frankie   Fuzzy   Feathers   Fergie

_____, _____, _____, _____

2   Which meaning of the word *kind* is used in the sentence below?

We love eating bread that the kind humans throw to us.

Ⓐ   caring and nice

Ⓑ   a sort or type

Ⓒ   a group of people

Ⓓ   in a way

3   Which word rhymes with *fight*?

Ⓐ   fort

Ⓑ   laugh

Ⓒ   mist

Ⓓ   white

4   What is the best way to combine the sentences below?

I live in a pond. The pond is in a park.

Ⓐ   I live in a pond park.

Ⓑ   I live in a pond in a park.

Ⓒ   I live in a pond, is in a park.

Ⓓ   I live in a pond and is in a park.

Quiz 9

Read the passage below. Then answer the questions that follow it.

Crying Over Onions

It is a well-known fact that chopping onions makes people cry. But why does this happen. There is actually a very good reason for this. It is not because onions make people sad!

Onions contain chemicals. When the onion skin is cut, the chemicals are released into the air. They are released as gases. The gases travel through the air. If the gas gets into your eyes, it causes them to sting. Your body makes you cry to help clean the gas from your eyes. This stops them from stinging. This is one way that the body can help care for itself. The next time your eyes water, don't be annoyed. Be glad that your body is looking after you.

1   The word *chopping* is the base word *chop* with the suffix *-ing* added. When the suffix is added, the *p* is doubled. For each word below, write the word with the suffix *-ing* added to it. Be sure to spell each word correctly.

stop   _____

skip   _____

cut   _____

run   _____

rub   _____

2   What is the correct way to end the sentence below?

But why does this happen.

Ⓐ   But why does this happen!

Ⓑ   But why does this happen?

Ⓒ   But why does this happen;

Ⓓ   It is correct as it is.

3   Read these sentences from the second paragraph.

Your body makes you cry to help clean the gas from your eyes. This stops them from stinging.

What does the word *them* in the second sentence refer to?

Ⓐ   the chemicals from the onion

Ⓑ   the person's eyes

Ⓒ   people who cut onions

Ⓓ   the layers of the onion

4   Which of these rewrites the last sentence with the most suitable transition word?

Ⓐ   However, be glad that your body is looking after you.

Ⓑ   Finally, be glad that your body is looking after you.

Ⓒ   Instead, be glad that your body is looking after you.

Ⓓ   Also, be glad that your body is looking after you.

Quiz 10

Read the passage below. Then answer the questions that follow it.

Bones

Bones are a very important part of the body. When a baby human is born, it has over 270 bones. Over time, many of the bones fuse to others. This makes a bone that is more large. Fully grown adult humans have about 206 bones. Bones are made of hard materials. The most important material is calcium.

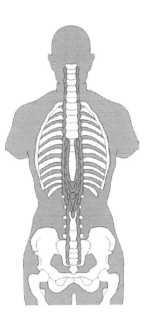

Humans put calcium into their bodies in many ways. One important way is by eating or drinking dairy products like milk and cheese. Calcium is also found in green vegetables like broccoli. Broccoli is easy to grow in a home garden. Calcium is also found in shellfish sardines and almonds. To have healthy bones, make sure your diet includes plenty of calcium.

1   In which sentence does the word *hard* have the same meaning as the sentence below?

     Bones are made of hard materials.

     Ⓐ   The test we took was quite hard.

     Ⓑ   I hurt myself when I fell on the hard ground.

     Ⓒ   The teacher can be hard on her students.

     Ⓓ   It was hard to run to the top of the steep hill.

2   What is the best way to rewrite the sentence below?

This makes a bone that is more large.

ⓐ   This makes a larger bone.

ⓑ   This make a largest bone.

ⓒ   This makes a more large bone.

ⓓ   This makes a more larger bone.

3   What is the correct way to use commas in the sentence below?

Calcium is also found in shellfish sardines and almonds.

ⓐ   Calcium is also found in shellfish sardines, and almonds.

ⓑ   Calcium is also found in shellfish, sardines, and almonds.

ⓒ   Calcium is also found in shellfish sardines, and, almonds.

ⓓ   Calcium is also found in shellfish, sardines, and, almonds.

4   Which sentence does NOT belong in the passage?

ⓐ   *When a baby human is born, it has over 270 bones.*

ⓑ   *The most important material is calcium.*

ⓒ   *One important way is by eating or drinking dairy products like milk and cheese.*

ⓓ   *Broccoli is easy to grow in a home garden.*

Revising and Editing Quizzes

Set 3

Instructions

Read each passage. Each passage is followed by questions.

For each multiple-choice question, read the question carefully. Then select the best answer. Fill in the circle for the correct answer.

For other types of questions, follow the instructions given.

Building Your Vocabulary

As you read the passages, list any words you do not understand below. Use a dictionary to look up the meaning of the word. Write the meaning of the word below.

Word: _____

Meaning: _____

_____

Word: _____

Meaning: _____

_____

Word: _____

Meaning: _____

_____

Word: _____

Meaning: _____

_____

Word: _____

Meaning: _____

_____

Quiz 11

Read the passage below. Then answer the questions that follow it.

Mother Knows Best

I wanted to eat my dinner in bed.
My mother said, "Eat at the table instead!"
I did not lissen. I should have thought twice.
Now my bedroom is home to two hungry mice!

1   Words that rhyme can have the same letters at the end. The words *twice* and *mice* are an example of this. Other rhyming words have different letters at the end. The words *bed* and *instead* are an example of this. For each set of words below, circle the two words that rhyme. Then write another rhyming word on the blank line.

| care | car | chair | cart | _____ |

| hope | cloak | soap | note | _____ |

| rain | ran | plant | plain | _____ |

| wart | start | sort | more | _____ |

| fit | night | write | rate | _____ |

2   Which word from the poem is an adjective, or describing word?

    Ⓐ   dinner

    Ⓑ   bed

    Ⓒ   thought

    Ⓓ   hungry

3   Which of these is the correct way to spell *lissen*?

    Ⓐ   lisen

    Ⓑ   lisan

    Ⓒ   lissan

    Ⓓ   listen

4   Which word from the poem is a compound word?

    Ⓐ   wanted

    Ⓑ   mother

    Ⓒ   table

    Ⓓ   bedroom

5   Which of these is the correct way to shorten "should have"?

    Ⓐ   should've

    Ⓑ   should'ave

    Ⓒ   shouldve'

    Ⓓ   shouldave'

Quiz 12

Read the passage below. Then answer the questions that follow it.

To the Moon

Dear Alex,

(1) I want to be an astronaut I have decided when I grow up. (2) They go up into space! (3) I want to bounce around on the Moon like Neil Armstrong. (4) He was the first person to walk on the Moon. (5) I think it would have been very exciting for him. (6) I think it might also have been a bit scary.

(7) If I left the Earth, I would probably feel scared. (8) I think it would be worth it. (9) I like the idea of looking back at the Earth from space. (10) I hope one day I can become an astronaut. (11) Dad keeps telling me that I will have to do well in math and science. (12) I know I will have to do more better in science.

Bye for now,

Jin

1   Where would be the best place to add the sentence below?

The Earth would look tiny from space.

   Ⓐ   After sentence 2

   Ⓑ   After sentence 6

   Ⓒ   After sentence 9

   Ⓓ   After sentence 11

2   Which sentence does the art in the passage best relate to?

    (A)   Sentence 7

    (B)   Sentence 9

    (C)   Sentence 10

    (D)   Sentence 11

3   Which of these is the best way to combine sentences 5 and 6?

    (A)   I think it would have been very exciting for him, but I think it might also have been a bit scary.

    (B)   I think it would have been very exciting and scary for him.

    (C)   I think it would have been very exciting, and a bit scary too, for him.

    (D)   I think it would have been very exciting for him, but a bit scary as well.

4   Which of these is the best way to rewrite sentence 1?

    (A)   I have decided that, when I grow up, I want to be an astronaut.

    (B)   I have decided that I want to be an astronaut when I grow up.

    (C)   When I grow up I have decided that I want to be an astronaut.

    (D)   I want to be when I grow up an astronaut, I have decided.

5   Which of these is the best way to rewrite sentence 12?

    (A)   I know I will have to do best in science.

    (B)   I know I will have to do gooder in science.

    (C)   I know I will have to do better in science.

    (D)   I know I will have to do more good in science.

Quiz 13

Read the passage below. Then answer the questions that follow it.

Animals of the Night

The sun has set. All of the birds is going to sleep. There is no longer the sound of chirping or singing. Many leafs float around. Blow down the city streets. The trees begin to sway in the wind.

Soon, the animals of the night will come out to play. The animals can be very loud. They may call out to each other. They will sometimes find a roof to run across. This sometimes wakes up sleeping humans. They wonder what the sound is above them. Then they drift off to sleep as the animals continue they're play.

1   The words *play* and *sway* both end with the letters *ay*. Choose the pairs of letters that can also be added to the start of *ay* to form a word. Write the words on the lines given.

st   th   cr   tr   bl   sc   cl   gr

_____ay   _____ay   _____ay   _____ay

2   Which sentence from the passage is NOT a complete sentence?

Ⓐ   *The sun has set.*

Ⓑ   *Blow down the city streets.*

Ⓒ   *They may call out to each other.*

Ⓓ   *This sometimes wakes up sleeping humans.*

3   Which change should be made in the second sentence?

Ⓐ   Change *of* to *off*

Ⓑ   Change *birds* to *bird*

Ⓒ   Change *is* to *are*

Ⓓ   Change *sleep* to *sleeps*

4   Which of these is the correct form of the plural of *leaf*?

Ⓐ   leaffs

Ⓑ   leafes

Ⓒ   leavs

Ⓓ   leaves

5   Which word should replace the word *they're* in the last sentence?

Ⓐ   there

Ⓑ   their

Ⓒ   they

Ⓓ   them

Quiz 14

Read the passage below. Then answer the questions that follow it.

Henry the Parrot

My pet is named Henry. Henry is a parrot. He enjoys eating seeds. He enjoys drinking water. When he is fed by my mother, he gets excited and flaps his wings.

One day, he was so excited that he spilled his water all over the floor! Then he stomped around in it. It was very amusing until I had to clean up the mess. Henry is the most great pet that I could ask for.

© Ruth Rogers

1   Complete the table by dividing the words listed below into one-syllable words and two-syllable words.

pet   parrot   enjoys   seeds   water

mother   wings   eating   clean   mess

One-Syllable Words	Two-Syllable Words

2   What is the best way to combine the sentences below?

He enjoys eating seeds. He enjoys drinking water.

Ⓐ   He enjoys eating seeds and drinking water.

Ⓑ   He enjoys eating and drinking seeds and water.

Ⓒ   He enjoys eating seeds, drinking water.

Ⓓ   He enjoys eating and drinking, seeds and water.

3   Which word or words should replace the words "most great" in the sentence below?

Henry is the most great pet that I could ask for.

Ⓐ   greater

Ⓑ   greatest

Ⓒ   more great

Ⓓ   most greatest

4   What is the best way to rewrite the first part of the sentence below?

When he is fed by my mother, he gets excited and flaps his wings.

Ⓐ   When by my mother he is fed,

Ⓑ   When feeds him my mother,

Ⓒ   When he is by my mother fed,

Ⓓ   When my mother feeds him,

Quiz 15

Read the passage below. Then answer the questions that follow it.

An Unusual Gift

Alexander Graham Bell was the man who invented the telephone. He was born in scotland in 1847. When Bell was born, he was not given a middle name. Unlike today, most childs did not get a middle name until they were older.

Alexander Bell was 11 years old when a middle name he got. The middle name of "Graham" was given to him as a gift for his 11th birthday. It seems like an unusual gift. It was not that unusual for the time.

1   Which change should be made in the sentence below?

Unlike today, most childs did not get a middle name until they were older.

   Ⓐ   Change *most* to *more*

   Ⓑ   Change *childs* to *children*

   Ⓒ   Change *were* to *was*

   Ⓓ   There is no change needed.

2 What does the prefix in the word *unusual* mean?

    Ⓐ   not

    Ⓑ   more

    Ⓒ   again

    Ⓓ   before

3 Which word from the passage should start with a capital letter?

    Ⓐ   Invented

    Ⓑ   Telephone

    Ⓒ   Scotland

    Ⓓ   Today

4 Which of these rewrites the last sentence with the most suitable transition word?

    Ⓐ   Again, it was not that unusual for the time.

    Ⓑ   Nearly, it was not that unusual for the time.

    Ⓒ   Finally, it was not that unusual for the time.

    Ⓓ   However, it was not that unusual for the time.

5 What is the best way to rewrite the first sentence of paragraph 2?

    Ⓐ   When a middle name he got, Alexander Bell was 11 years old.

    Ⓑ   Alexander Bell, when a middle name he got, was 11 years old.

    Ⓒ   Alexander Bell was 11 years old when he got a middle name.

    Ⓓ   When he got a middle name, 11 years old Alexander Bell was.

Revising and Editing Quizzes

Set 4

Instructions

Read each passage. Each passage is followed by questions.

For each multiple-choice question, read the question carefully. Then select the best answer. Fill in the circle for the correct answer.

For other types of questions, follow the instructions given.

Building Your Vocabulary

As you read the passages, list any words you do not understand below. Use a dictionary to look up the meaning of the word. Write the meaning of the word below.

Word: _____

Meaning: _____

_____

Word: _____

Meaning: _____

_____

Word: _____

Meaning: _____

_____

Word: _____

Meaning: _____

_____

Word: _____

Meaning: _____

_____

Quiz 16

Read the passage below. Then answer the questions that follow it.

Turtles

Turtles is the only reptiles that have shells. Turtles use their shells for protection. They pull their heads arms and legs inside of their shell. Most turtles live in fresh water.

Like all reptiles, turtles lay eggs. If a turtle lives mostly on land, it is known as a tortoise. They look different from turtles. They will often be much bigger in size. Turtles can be a lot of fun to watch swim in a pond. Some people even keep turtles as pets.

©Jonathan Zander

1   Which change should be made in the first sentence?

    Ⓐ   Change *is* to *are*

    Ⓑ   Change *that* to *those*

    Ⓒ   Change *have* to *had*

    Ⓓ   There is no change needed.

2   Which word in the sentence below is a verb, or an action word?

    Most turtles live in fresh water.

    Ⓐ   turtles

    Ⓑ   live

    Ⓒ   fresh

    Ⓓ   water

3 Which sentence would be best to add to the beginning of the passage to state the central idea?

Ⓐ   It is rare to see a turtle.

Ⓑ   There is no need to fear turtles.

Ⓒ   Turtles are interesting animals.

Ⓓ   Turtles eat plants and insects.

4 Which of these is a way to rewrite the sentence below without changing the meaning of the sentence?

They will often be much bigger in size.

Ⓐ   They will often be much bigger.

Ⓑ   They will be much bigger in size.

Ⓒ   They will often be in size.

Ⓓ   They will often be bigger.

5 Which of these shows the correct use of commas in the sentence below?

They pull their heads arms and legs inside of their shell.

Ⓐ   They pull, their heads arms and legs, inside of their shell.

Ⓑ   They pull their heads arms and legs, inside of their shell.

Ⓒ   They pull their heads, arms, and legs inside of their shell.

Ⓓ   They pull their heads, arms, and legs, inside of their shell.

Quiz 17

Read the passage below. Then answer the questions that follow it.

Fish Food

"Come on, it's not that far now!" Sam yelled.

Ben wipe away some sweat and kept going. It was a very warm day, and it just kept getting warmer. Sam and Ben were on their way to the big lake to catch some fish. They had their fishing rods and some bait to put on their hooks.

They finally found a good spot near the lake. They sat down to start fishing. Ben opened the ice cream container where he had asked his mother to put the bait.

"This is not fishing bait. These worms are made of candy!" Ben said. "I should have told Mom I wanted worms to use as bait."

"We could still try," Sam offered. "Maybe the fish will like the candy worms."

Ben wasn't sure it would work. It sounded like fun.

"It's worth a try," Ben said.

1   Rewrite each sentence by placing the quotation marks in the correct place.

Where are you going? Rachel asked.

_____

I am busy right now, Kyra said.

_____

2   What is the correct way to rewrite the second sentence?

  Ⓐ   Ben wiped away some sweat and kept going.

  Ⓑ   Ben wiping away some sweat and kept going.

  Ⓒ   Ben was wiped away some sweat and kept going.

  Ⓓ   Ben will wipe away some sweat and kept going.

3   Which change should be made in the sentence below?

  Sam and Ben were on their way to the big lake to catch some fish.

  Ⓐ   Change *were* to *where*

  Ⓑ   Change *their* to *there*

  Ⓒ   Change *some* to *sum*

  Ⓓ   There is no change needed.

4   Which of these shows the correct word to use when connecting the sentences below?

  Ben wasn't sure it would work. It sounded like fun.

  Ⓐ   Ben wasn't sure it would work, so it sounded like fun.

  Ⓑ   Ben wasn't sure it would work, or it sounded like fun.

  Ⓒ   Ben wasn't sure it would work, but it sounded like fun.

  Ⓓ   Ben wasn't sure it would work, and it sounded like fun.

Quiz 18

Read the passage below. Then answer the questions that follow it.

Sports Day

(1) Today is the day my class plays sport. (2) Our teacher asked us which sport we wanted to play. (3) I said I wanted to play football the mostest. (4) My friend Ling said he wanted to play baseball. (5) It seemed like everyone had different ideas.

(6) The teacher asked everyone in the class to choose between football, baseball, and basketball. (7) The teacher added up how many votes there were for each sport. (8) We ended up playing basketball. (9) Our teacher said that it was only fair that we played basketball.

(10) I still wish we could have played football. (11) However, I think it was a fair way to choose. (12) Still fun playing basketball.

1   A compound word is a word made by adding together two different words. The words *football*, *baseball*, and *basketball* are compound words. Each word ends with the word *ball*. For each set below, write three compounds words with the word part shown.

book_____   book_____   book_____

door_____   door_____   door_____

_____man   _____man   _____man

2   Where would be the best place to add the sentence below?

The teacher kept a tally of the votes.

    Ⓐ   Before sentence 6

    Ⓑ   After sentence 6

    Ⓒ   After sentence 8

    Ⓓ   After sentence 9

3   Which sentence from the passage is NOT a complete sentence?

    Ⓐ   Sentence 1

    Ⓑ   Sentence 3

    Ⓒ   Sentence 10

    Ⓓ   Sentence 12

4   Which sentence would best follow sentence 12 to end the passage?

    Ⓐ   Our teacher can be hard to talk to.

    Ⓑ   I have a lot of friends at school.

    Ⓒ   Maybe next time we will play football.

    Ⓓ   I am not very good at baseball.

5   Which change should be made in sentence 3?

    Ⓐ   Change *said* to *says*

    Ⓑ   Change *play* to *plays*

    Ⓒ   Change *mostest* to *most*

    Ⓓ   There is no change needed.

Quiz 19

Read the passage below. Then answer the questions that follow it.

Basketball

Basketball is a game that have ten players divided into two teams. This means that each team has five players. To play basketball, you bounce a ball and score points by throwing the ball into the basket.

There is a basket at the top of a post on each side of the cort. Each team has a basket to keep safe from the other team. Some people for their career play basketball. Most of those players are above 6 feet tall.

1   In the passage, the word *post* means "a pole." Write another meaning for the word *post* on the lines below.

_____

_____

In the passage, the word *feet* means "a unit of measure." Write another meaning for the word *feet* on the lines below.

_____

_____

2   Which change should be made in the first sentence?

Ⓐ   Change *have* to *has*

Ⓑ   Change *players* to *player's*

Ⓒ   Change *two* to *too*

Ⓓ   There is no change needed.

3   What is the correct way to spell *cort*?

Ⓐ   corte

Ⓑ   coert

Ⓒ   coart

Ⓓ   court

4   What is the best way to rewrite the sentence below?

Some people for their career play basketball.

Ⓐ   Some people play basketball for their career.

Ⓑ   For their career, some people play basketball.

Ⓒ   Play basketball, some people do, for their career.

Ⓓ   Do play basketball for their career some people.

5   Which word should replace *above* in the last sentence?

Ⓐ   almost

Ⓑ   about

Ⓒ   around

Ⓓ   over

Quiz 20

Read the passage below. Then answer the questions that follow it.

Jupiter

Jupiter is the fifth planet from the Sun. It is the largest planet in the Solar System. Jupiter is made up of gases. It does not have a hard crust like the Earth does. This means that there is no solid place for a spaceship or rocket to land. This makes it difficult for scientists to study Jupiter. But scientists have found a way.

Scientists have sent a special camera to study Jupiter. The camera is circling the gas planet. It is in orbit around Jupiter. The camera takes photos of many things. It has taken photos of the sixteen moons around Jupiter.

1   Nouns are words that name people, places, things, or ideas. Proper nouns name a certain person, place, or thing. Proper nouns start with capital letters. Complete the table below by listing three more nouns and three more proper nouns from the passage.

Nouns	Proper Nouns
planet	Jupiter

2 Which two words from the passage have about the same meaning?

    Ⓐ   hard, solid

    Ⓑ   gases, crust

    Ⓒ   spaceship, scientists

    Ⓓ   camera, photos

3 What is the correct way to spell the past tense of *study*?

    Ⓐ   studyed

    Ⓑ   studied

    Ⓒ   studdied

    Ⓓ   studded

4 What does the word *largest* mean?

    Ⓐ   was large

    Ⓑ   less large

    Ⓒ   more large

    Ⓓ   the most large

5 What is the correct way to shorten the words "does not"?

    Ⓐ   doesnt

    Ⓑ   does'nt

    Ⓒ   doesn't

    Ⓓ   doesnt'

Section 2
Language, Vocabulary, and Grammar Quizzes

Instructions

For each multiple-choice question, read the question carefully. Then select the best answer. Fill in the circle for the correct answer.

For other types of questions, follow the instructions given.

Quiz 21: Analyze Words

1   The word *neck* ends in *eck*. Which letter can be added to *eck* to form another word?

    Ⓐ   d

    Ⓑ   m

    Ⓒ   s

    Ⓓ   t

2   Which pair of letters can be placed before the letters below to form a word?

                           ____ing

    Ⓐ   tw

    Ⓑ   sh

    Ⓒ   st

    Ⓓ   pr

3   Which word rhymes with *sail*?

    Ⓐ   will

    Ⓑ   school

    Ⓒ   while

    Ⓓ   male

4   Which word does NOT rhyme with the three other words?

    Ⓐ   poor

    Ⓑ   war

    Ⓒ   store

    Ⓓ   car

Quiz 22: Write and Spell Words Correctly

Circle the correct way to write the name of the object shown in each picture.

1   bear   bare

2   shepe   sheep

3   bote   boat

4   goat   gote

5   bred   bread

6   plain   plane

7   clock   clok

8   coyn   coin

Quiz 23: Identify Correct Spellings

Circle the correct way to write each color below.

1	white	wight	whyte
2	bloo	bleu	blue
3	grene	green	grean
4	red	read	rede

Circle the correct way to write each fruit below.

5	pare	pear	pair
6	peech	peich	peach
7	lime	lyme	liem
8	graip	grape	graep

Circle the correct way to write each animal below.

9	whail	whale	wale	wail
10	toad	tode	toed	toade
11	sele	seel	seal	siel
12	gouse	gose	goos	goose

Quiz 24: Place Words in Alphabetical Order

1   Which word would go first in alphabetical order?

Ⓐ   storm

Ⓑ   start

Ⓒ   stir

Ⓓ   string

2   Which set of words are in alphabetical order?

Ⓐ   pair, pear, poke

Ⓑ   pair, poke, pear

Ⓒ   poke, pear, pair

Ⓓ   pear, pair, poke

3   Using alphabetical order, which word could go between the words?

clap, _____, clown

Ⓐ   chop

Ⓑ   clean

Ⓒ   crown

Ⓓ   clue

4   List the words below in alphabetical order.

train   three   twist   tiger

_____, _____, _____, _____

Quiz 25: Divide Words into Syllables

For each word below, divide the word into two syllables. The first one has been completed for you.

1	monkey	mon / key
2	before	_____
3	circus	_____
4	happy	_____
5	letter	_____
6	never	_____
7	window	_____
8	yellow	_____

For each word below, divide the word into three syllables. The first one has been completed for you.

9	elephant	el / e / phant
10	afternoon	_____
11	family	_____
12	telephone	_____
13	tomorrow	_____
14	wonderful	_____

Quiz 26: Understand and Use Abbreviations

Addresses often include abbreviations. Write the correct abbreviation for each address below.

1   2265 Second Avenue   2265 Second _____

2   180 Main Road   180 Main _____

3   35 Smith Street   35 Smith _____

4   11 Greenway Drive   11 Greenway _____

Titles used for people are often abbreviated, or written in a shorter form. Write the correct abbreviations for each title below.

5   William Carter Junior   William Carter _____

6   Mister John Logan   _____ John Logan

7   Doctor Marie Diaz   _____ Marie Diaz

Write the correct abbreviation for each unit of measure below.

8   foot   _____

9   yard   _____

10   ounce   _____

11   pound   _____

12   centimeter   _____

Quiz 27: Identify and Use Antonyms

1   Which word means the opposite of *tall*?

    Ⓐ   high

    Ⓑ   short

    Ⓒ   big

    Ⓓ   nice

2   Which word does NOT have the same meaning as the others?

    Ⓐ   neat

    Ⓑ   clean

    Ⓒ   messy

    Ⓓ   tidy

3   Which word means the opposite of *dark*?

    Ⓐ   light

    Ⓑ   nice

    Ⓒ   dim

    Ⓓ   scary

4   Which two words have opposite meanings?

    Ⓐ   bright, idea

    Ⓑ   rich, great

    Ⓒ   kind, nasty

    Ⓓ   wide, broad

Quiz 28: Identify Base Words

1   What is the base word of *taking*?

    Ⓐ   tak

    Ⓑ   take

    Ⓒ   king

    Ⓓ   ing

2   What is the base word of *trainer*?

    Ⓐ   tra

    Ⓑ   er

    Ⓒ   rain

    Ⓓ   train

3   What is the base word of *friendship*?

    Ⓐ   fri

    Ⓑ   friend

    Ⓒ   end

    Ⓓ   ship

4   What is the base word of *beautiful*?

    Ⓐ   beau

    Ⓑ   beauty

    Ⓒ   iful

    Ⓓ   ful

Quiz 29: Use Plurals Correctly

For each question below, complete each sentence by adding the correct word to the sentence.

1   We had a _____ in the park.   picnic   picnics

2   I washed all the _____ of the car.   window   windows

3   My house is at the end of the _____.   street   streets

4   I share a _____ with my sister.   room   rooms

5   I drank two _____ of water.   bottle   bottles

6   Sam and I both got new _____.   bike   bikes

7   That_____ is a hundred years old.   clock   clocks

8   There was a huge pile of _____.   leafs   leaves

9   I have a pet _____ named Randy.   mouse   mice

10 They say that cats have nine _____.   lifes   lives

Quiz 30: Identify Proper Nouns

Proper nouns start with a capital letter. For each question below, identify the proper noun in the sentence. Then rewrite the sentence with the proper noun capitalized.

1   Many people like to sleep in on sunday.

_____

2   It rained a lot last june.

_____

3   My sister sarah is older than me.

_____

4   It took hours to get to florida.

_____

5   It would be nice to visit canada one day.

_____

6   These shoes came from walmart.

_____

Quiz 31: Use Words with Suffixes

For each question below, select the word that correctly completes the sentence.

1   The attic was very _____.

    Ⓐ   mess

    Ⓑ   messy

    Ⓒ   messier

    Ⓓ   messiest

2   Trevor _____ walked on the sharp rocks.

    Ⓐ   carefully

    Ⓑ   careful

    Ⓒ   careless

    Ⓓ   caring

3   Skye and Brooke have a strong _____.

    Ⓐ   friendly

    Ⓑ   friends

    Ⓒ   friendship

    Ⓓ   friendless

4   The _____ of the sheep's wool was surprising.

    Ⓐ   softness

    Ⓑ   softer

    Ⓒ   softly

    Ⓓ   soften

Quiz 32: Spell Commonly Misspelled Words

For each question below, circle the word in the sentence that is spelled incorrectly. Write the correct spelling of the word on the line.

1   My favrite time of year is summer.

_____

2   I have only a few close frends.

_____

3   I allways read before going to sleep.

_____

4   Kim sed she wanted to buy a new book.

_____

5   I met some new peeple at school today.

_____

6   It is quite common to be scarred of spiders.

_____

Quiz 33: Understand and Use Prefixes

1   What does the word *restart* mean?

    Ⓐ   not start

    Ⓑ   start again

    Ⓒ   start before

    Ⓓ   start after

2   Which prefix can be added to the word *kind* to make a word meaning "not kind"?

    Ⓐ   un-

    Ⓑ   re-

    Ⓒ   mis-

    Ⓓ   pre-

3   Which prefix should be added to the word to make the sentence correct?

Phil never eats peas because he __likes them.

    Ⓐ   un-

    Ⓑ   dis-

    Ⓒ   re-

    Ⓓ   mis-

4   A television that has been *preset* has been

    Ⓐ   set well

    Ⓑ   set badly

    Ⓒ   set after

    Ⓓ   set before

Quiz 34: Understand and Use Suffixes

1   What does the word *coolest* mean?

     Ⓐ   in a way that is cool

     Ⓑ   the most cool

     Ⓒ   less cool

     Ⓓ   more cool

2   Which suffix can be added to the word *hope* to make a word meaning "without hope"?

     Ⓐ   -ful

     Ⓑ   -ing

     Ⓒ   -less

     Ⓓ   -ed

3   Which word makes the sentence correct?

     The yellow wall made the room look bright and _____.

     Ⓐ   coloring

     Ⓑ   colorful

     Ⓒ   colorless

     Ⓓ   colorer

4   Which word means "the most nice"?

     Ⓐ   nicer

     Ⓑ   nicest

     Ⓒ   nicely

     Ⓓ   niceness

Quiz 35: Spell Words with Suffixes Correctly

1   Which underlined word is spelled incorrectly?

    Ⓐ   <u>hopping</u> on one leg

    Ⓑ   <u>jumping</u> up and down

    Ⓒ   <u>joging</u> around the block

    Ⓓ   <u>running</u> down the path

2   Which underlined word is spelled incorrectly?

    Ⓐ   <u>played</u> a game

    Ⓑ   <u>walked</u> home

    Ⓒ   <u>waitted</u> a long time

    Ⓓ   <u>helped</u> a friend

3   Which word is spelled incorrectly?

    Ⓐ   tidyed

    Ⓑ   painted

    Ⓒ   wished

    Ⓓ   skipped

4   Which underlined word is spelled incorrectly?

    Ⓐ   <u>catches</u> a ball

    Ⓑ   <u>sleeps</u> at night

    Ⓒ   <u>watchs</u> the rain

    Ⓓ   <u>counts</u> the coins

Quiz 36: Use Contractions

A contraction is a shortened form of two words. For example, *I am* can be shortened to *I'm*. For each question below, write the contraction for the two words given. Then write a sentence that uses the contraction.

1   you are   _____

_____

2   he will   _____

_____

3   that is   _____

_____

4   is not   _____

_____

5   you have   _____

_____

6   did not   _____

_____

Quiz 37: Identify and Use Synonyms

1 Which word means about the same as *shut* in the sentence below?

The teacher asked Sandy to shut the door.

- Ⓐ slam
- Ⓑ close
- Ⓒ open
- Ⓓ send

2 Which two words have about the same meaning?

- Ⓐ shiny, dull
- Ⓑ story, tale
- Ⓒ wrap, rap
- Ⓓ cheerful, sad

3 Which word means about the same as *finish*?

- Ⓐ start
- Ⓑ finally
- Ⓒ end
- Ⓓ begin

4 Which word does NOT mean the same as the other three words?

- Ⓐ merry
- Ⓑ sad
- Ⓒ happy
- Ⓓ cheerful

Quiz 38: Identify Types of Words

Verbs are action words. Adjectives are describing words. Identify the verb and the adjective in each sentence below.

1   Harry ran quickly down the road.

   Verb _____   Adjective   _____

2   We finally won the close game.

   Verb _____   Adjective   _____

3   I baked a beautiful cake.

   Verb _____   Adjective   _____

4   Margo washed the dirty clothes.

   Verb _____   Adjective   _____

5   The dress I bought is too large.

   Verb _____   Adjective   _____

6   The grass looked green after the rain.

   Verb _____   Adjective   _____

Quiz 39: Use Correct Verb Tense

For each question below, choose the correct verb tense to complete the sentence.

1   I _____ my story tomorrow.

    Ⓐ   writes

    Ⓑ   wrote

    Ⓒ   was writing

    Ⓓ   will write

2   We _____ ten laps of the pool yesterday.

    Ⓐ   swim

    Ⓑ   swam

    Ⓒ   was swimming

    Ⓓ   will swim

3   Yesterday, I _____ over and hurt myself.

    Ⓐ   trip

    Ⓑ   tripped

    Ⓒ   has tripped

    Ⓓ   will trip

4   I often _____ to school by myself.

    Ⓐ   walk

    Ⓑ   walks

    Ⓒ   was walking

    Ⓓ   has walked

Quiz 40: Use Pronouns

For each question below, choose the pronoun that best completes the sentence.

1   Andrew made _____ bed.

     Ⓐ   him

     Ⓑ   its

     Ⓒ   he

     Ⓓ   his

2   I wrote a letter and posted _____.

     Ⓐ   it

     Ⓑ   him

     Ⓒ   her

     Ⓓ   them

3   That dog belongs to me. That is _____ dog.

     Ⓐ   me

     Ⓑ   my

     Ⓒ   mine

     Ⓓ   him

4   We won a ribbon for _____ school project.

     Ⓐ   us

     Ⓑ   them

     Ⓒ   our

     Ⓓ   it

Quiz 41: Use Words to Show Time Order

For each question below, choose the word or phrase that best completes the sentence.

1   _____ you frost the cake, make sure you let it cool down first.

   Ⓐ   Earlier

   Ⓑ   After

   Ⓒ   Before

   Ⓓ   While

2   _____, Julie felt scared. Then she began to feel better.

   Ⓐ   At first

   Ⓑ   Finally

   Ⓒ   In the end

   Ⓓ   At the same time

3   Don't sit on the chair we painted _____ the paint has dried.

   Ⓐ   while

   Ⓑ   until

   Ⓒ   after

   Ⓓ   then

4   We waited at the bus stop for a long time. _____, the bus arrived.

   Ⓐ   Meanwhile

   Ⓑ   Earlier

   Ⓒ   First of all

   Ⓓ   At last

Quiz 42: Understand Word Meanings

1   What does the word *empty* show about the room?

Wendy was surprised to see that the room was empty.

Ⓐ   It was small.

Ⓑ   It had nothing in it.

Ⓒ   It was quiet.

Ⓓ   It smelled odd.

2   Which word in the sentence tells when the events take place?

The chilly evening air made the students shiver.

Ⓐ   chilly

Ⓑ   evening

Ⓒ   students

Ⓓ   shiver

3   What does the word *frighten* mean in the sentence below?

Joel wanted to sneak up on Carly and frighten her.

Ⓐ   wake

Ⓑ   mean

Ⓒ   scare

Ⓓ   shout

Quiz 43: Spell Words Correctly

1   Which underlined word is spelled incorrectly?

Ⓐ   fourth quarter

Ⓑ   feeling angry

Ⓒ   one dollar

Ⓓ   librery book

2   Which underlined word is spelled incorrectly?

Ⓐ   major problem

Ⓑ   lemon juice

Ⓒ   magic trick

Ⓓ   large jiant

3   Which underlined word is spelled incorrectly?

Ⓐ   twelve months

Ⓑ   middle of the night

Ⓒ   luky number

Ⓓ   bounce the ball

4   Which underlined word is spelled incorrectly?

Ⓐ   light as a feather

Ⓑ   in the begginning

Ⓒ   around the corner

Ⓓ   get a second chance

Quiz 44: Use Correct Punctuation

1   Which sentence has correct punctuation?

    Ⓐ   The stars are bright tonight,

    Ⓑ   Do you know what that star is?

    Ⓒ   There is a very cold breeze?

    Ⓓ   Do you like looking up at the stars.

2   Which underlined word is written correctly?

    Ⓐ   The <u>cat's</u> always have water.

    Ⓑ   The <u>teacher's</u> desk is new.

    Ⓒ   The <u>shop's</u> are closed tonight.

    Ⓓ   The <u>boy's</u> waited for their bus.

3   Which underlined word is written correctly?

    Ⓐ   It <u>is'nt</u> too late.

    Ⓑ   We <u>couldv'e</u> waited longer.

    Ⓒ   They <u>aren't</u> sure what happened.

    Ⓓ   <u>Iv'e</u> never seen her before.

4   Complete each sentence by adding one of the punctuation marks below.

.   ?   !

Have you seen Amy anywhere____

We have to go right now_____

It was a long and boring day_____

Quiz 45: Identify Base Words and Suffixes

For each question below, write the base word and the suffix on the lines.

1   driving

   Base word: _____   Suffix: _____

2   talked

   Base word: _____   Suffix: _____

3   stopped

   Base word: _____   Suffix: _____

4   pulling

   Base word: _____   Suffix: _____

5   makes

   Base word: _____   Suffix: _____

6   smiled

   Base word: _____   Suffix: _____

Quiz 46: Use Homophones

1   In which sentence are the underlined words used correctly?

     Ⓐ   The <u>bare</u> <u>ate</u> a fish.

     Ⓑ   The <u>bear</u> <u>ate</u> a fish.

     Ⓒ   The <u>bare</u> <u>eight</u> a fish.

     Ⓓ   The <u>bear</u> <u>eight</u> a fish.

2   In which sentence is the underlined word used correctly?

     Ⓐ   I like playing baseball <u>to</u>.

     Ⓑ   I like playing baseball <u>too</u>.

     Ⓒ   I like playing baseball <u>tow</u>.

     Ⓓ   I like playing baseball <u>two</u>.

3   In which sentence is the underlined word used correctly?

     Ⓐ   Fiona does not like to <u>were</u> dresses.

     Ⓑ   Fiona does not like to <u>ware</u> dresses.

     Ⓒ   Fiona does not like to <u>wear</u> dresses.

     Ⓓ   Fiona does not like to <u>where</u> dresses.

4   In which sentence are the underlined words used correctly?

     Ⓐ   We were asked to <u>meat</u> near the <u>shoo</u> store.

     Ⓑ   We were asked to <u>meat</u> near the <u>shoe</u> store.

     Ⓒ   We were asked to <u>meet</u> near the <u>shoo</u> store.

     Ⓓ   We were asked to <u>meet</u> near the <u>shoe</u> store.

Quiz 47: Use Homographs

Homographs are words that are spelled the same, but have different meanings. For example, the word *bill* can mean "a piece of paper money" or can mean "a beak." For each word below, write two sentences using the word. Use a different meaning of the word in each sentence.

1   bat   1. _____

2. _____

2   park   1. _____

2. _____

3   rock   1. _____

2. _____

4   wave   1. _____

2. _____

5   light   1. _____

2. _____

Quiz 48: Use Correct Subject-Verb Agreement

For each question below, choose the word that best completes the sentence.

1   It _____ getting late, so I went to bed.

    Ⓐ   was

    Ⓑ   were

    Ⓒ   is

    Ⓓ   are

2   Jamie _____ too much.

    Ⓐ   talk

    Ⓑ   talks

    Ⓒ   talker

    Ⓓ   talking

3   The dogs _____ playing in the yard.

    Ⓐ   am

    Ⓑ   is

    Ⓒ   was

    Ⓓ   are

4   They _____ to be home before dark.

    Ⓐ   is

    Ⓑ   was

    Ⓒ   has

    Ⓓ   have

Section 3
Guided Writing Tasks

INTRODUCTION
For Parents, Teachers, and Tutors

Writing Skills

Students in grade 4 develop writing skills by producing writing for different purposes. There are three main writing purposes covered in grade 4. Part 3 of this book has one section for each type of writing.

- Writing to entertain – students write fictional stories based on a prompt
- Writing to describe – students write a personal narrative describing an experience or event
- Writing to explain – students write an essay explaining something or giving their opinion on a set topic

Preparing for the SOL Writing Test

The SOL Writing test taken by grade 5 students contains either a narrative writing prompt or an expository writing prompt. The writing tasks in the "Writing to Entertain" section will prepare students for a narrative writing prompt. Expository writing is writing that communicates ideas or information. The writing tasks in the "Writing to Describe" and "Writing to Explain" sections will prepare students for an expository writing prompt.

Hints

Each writing task includes a hint. Each hint is designed to have students focus on one area that will help them achieve good results in written tasks. After completing all five tasks, students will have developed key skills that will help ensure they score well on future writing tasks.

Planning

Planning is the key to having students produce writing that is clear, focused, and effective. For each writing task, students should follow the instructions for planning their writing and write a plan for their story or essay before they begin writing.

Writing to Entertain – Introduction

In these writing tasks, you are asked to write a story. Each writing task gives you a writing prompt to use as the starting point of your story. You should write a complete story with a beginning, middle, and end based on the writing prompt.

Good writers plan their stories before they start writing. Follow the steps below to plan your story.

Step 1
Read the writing prompt and think of an idea for your story. You may want to list several possible ideas. Choose one of these ideas to write about.

Step 2
Once you have decided on your idea, write a short statement describing what your story is about.

Step 3
Describe what is going to happen at the start of your story. At the start of the story, you might want to describe the main character and the main problem.

Step 4
Describe what is going to happen in the middle of your story. In the middle of a story, a problem might get worse or a key event might occur.

Step 5
Describe what is going to happen at the end of your story. The ending should solve the main problem.

Step 6
Start writing! Follow your plan as you write.

Step 7
After you have finished, check your work. Check your work for spelling, punctuation, and capitalization.

Writing to Entertain – Writing Task 1

Dani looked everywhere in the house for her backpack. It was nowhere to be found. She couldn't imagine where it might have gone.

Write a story about Dani's search for her backpack.

Hint

The writing prompt tells you that your story should be about the search for the backpack. Use this as the starting point and think of a story based around this idea. The beginning of the story will be that Dani is searching for her backpack. What happens after that is up to you!

You could have anything happen during the search. Maybe Dani discovers that a monkey has run off with the backpack. Maybe Dani's brother has hidden it. Maybe Dani puts together a search team. Be creative and try to make your story interesting!

Writing to Entertain – Writing Task 2

It was meant to be a relaxing picnic with friends. It did not turn out like that.

Write a story about what happened on the picnic.

Hint

A good story has a beginning, middle, and end. As you plan your story, focus on what is going to happen in each part.

The beginning often introduces the characters and the setting. The start of this story might describe the friends enjoying the picnic.

The middle of the story might describe what goes wrong. This will be the main part of your story. It will usually be 2 or 3 paragraphs long. In this part, describe the events that take place.

At the end of the story, the problem is usually solved. This ties up the story and makes it a complete story.

Writing to Entertain – Writing Task 3

Look at the picture below.

Write a story based on what is happening in the picture.

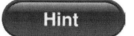

Your story should be based on the picture given. You should use the picture to come up with an idea for your story. The story shows a marching band. You could use a character that is in the marching band, or someone watching the marching band. Make sure you come up with a complete story based on a marching band.

The key to writing a good story based on a picture is not to focus on describing what is happening in the picture. Instead, use the picture as a general idea, and make sure you come up with a complete story based on a race.

Writing to Entertain – Writing Task 4

Look at the picture below.

Write a story based on what is happening in the picture.

One way to write a good story is to choose a style of writing and stick to it. You might choose to make your story funny, serious, or you might write a mystery story. If you choose a style and stick to it all through your story, it will be more interesting to the reader.

Writing to Entertain – Writing Task 5

Jamie lived next door to an inventor. One day, the inventor asked Jamie to help him. The inventor was working on a special new machine.

Write a story about the machine that the inventor is working on and how Jamie helps him.

Hint

One way to improve your writing is to focus on how you describe things. You can choose words and phrases that make your writing more interesting. Imagine that you want to describe the inventor's machine. Instead of saying it is very large, you might say that it looked like a giant metal monster. Instead of saying that it sounded loud, you might say that it rattled, shook, and roared.

By describing things in a more interesting way, you will make your story more interesting to the reader.

Writing to Describe – Introduction

In these writing tasks, you are asked to describe a personal experience. Each writing task will give you a topic. You then have to write about a personal experience on that topic.

In these tasks, you can use your own opinion. You can write about what happened, how you felt, or what you think about something now.

Before you start writing, plan what you are going to write. Follow the steps below to plan your writing.

Step 1
Start by thinking about the topic. Think about what you are going to write about. You may want to write a list of possible ideas. Choose one of these ideas to write about.

Step 2
Write a short summary of what you are going to write about.

Step 3
Read the writing prompt again and make sure what you are going to write about matches the writing prompt.

Step 4
Write a plan of what you are going to write. Write down the main points you want to make, and the order you are going to cover them.

Step 5
Start writing! Follow your plan as you write.

Step 6
After you have finished, check your work. Check your work for spelling, punctuation, and capitalization.

Writing to Describe – Writing Task 1

Think about a time when you achieved a goal. What was your goal and how did it feel to achieve it?

Write a composition describing a time when you achieved a goal. Describe what the goal was, why it was important to you, and how it felt to achieve it.

Hint

Make sure you answer each part of the question. Remember that you need to include the following:

- what the goal was
- why the goal was important to you
- how it felt to achieve it

When you write your outline, make sure that it covers all of the parts of the question.

Writing to Describe – Writing Task 2

Most people have a special event they look forward to each year. It might be a birthday, a family event, or a holiday. What special event do you look forward to?

Write a composition describing a special event that you look forward to. Explain why that event is special to you.

Hint

Stay focused! You might be able to think of many different events you could write about, but don't try to write about them all. Instead, choose just one event and write about that event in detail.

Your answer should describe the event. You should include many details that will help the reader imagine the event. Your answer should also explain why you look forward to the event and what makes it special.

Writing to Describe – Writing Task 3

Spiders

Some people say that I'm scary,
It makes my feelings kind of sore.
What they really need to know,
Is that *they* scare me even more!

In "Spiders," the poet describes how some people are afraid of spiders. What are you afraid of? How does being afraid affect you? Write a composition about what you are afraid of and how being afraid affects you.

Hint

This writing task introduces the topic by using a poem. You do not have to refer to the poem in your answer. The poem is just there to help you start thinking about the topic. The goal of your writing is to write about what you are scared of. You should also clearly describe how being scared affects you. You might describe how you feel and what you do when you are scared.

Writing to Describe – Writing Task 4

It can be hard to make new friends. Think about a time when you made a new friend.

Write a composition describing a time when you made a new friend. Explain whether it was hard or easy to make a new friend.

Hint

When planning your writing, it is a good idea to break down what you want to say into paragraphs. This will help make sure your writing is well-organized and easy to understand. In your outline, describe what you are going to cover in each paragraph. Make sure that each paragraph has one main idea.

Writing to Describe – Writing Task 5

Most people look forward to summer vacations. What do you look forward to most about summer vacations?

Write a composition describing what you look forward to most about summer vacations.

<table>
<tr><td>

Hint

When writing compositions like this, you should focus on 2 or 3 things that you like most about summer vacations. There may be many more things that you like. However, it is better to describe 2 or 3 things in detail than to list many things you like. You will be scored on how well you describe what you like about summer vacations, not on how many things you can think of!

When you write your plan, choose the 2 or 3 things you like most and write one paragraph about each thing.

</td></tr>
</table>

Writing to Explain – Introduction

In these writing tasks, you are asked to give your opinion on a topic. Each task will give you a topic to think about. You have to decide what your opinion is. Then you have to explain what your opinion is and why. You should use facts, details, or examples to support your opinion.

Before you start writing, plan what you are going to write. Follow the steps below to plan your writing.

Step 1
Start by thinking about the topic. Decide what your opinion is on the topic.

Step 2
Write a short summary of what you are going to write about.

Step 3
Read the writing prompt again and make sure what you are going to write about matches the writing prompt.

Step 4
List the facts, details, or examples you are going to use to support your opinion.

Step 5
Write a plan of what you are going to write. Write down the main points you want to make, and the order you are going to cover them.

Step 6
Start writing! Follow your plan as you write.

Step 7
After you have finished, check your work. Check your work for spelling, punctuation, and capitalization.

Writing to Explain – Writing Task 1

Some people believe that it is very important to be on time. They think it is very rude to be late.

Do you think it is very important to be on time? Why or why not? Use facts, details, or examples to support your opinion.

Hint

You may have several different opinions. Maybe you think it is rude to be late. However, you might also think that sometimes it cannot be helped. A good composition will have one clear idea. Even if you have several ideas, choose one to focus on in your writing. It is better to support one opinion very well than to describe many different opinions!

Writing to Explain – Writing Task 2

Read this proverb about actions.

Actions speak louder than words.

Explain what this proverb means to you. Use facts, details, or examples in your answer.

Hint

A proverb is a short saying that states an idea. The idea in this proverb is that actions are more important than words. In your writing, you should write about how this proverb relates to you. Your answer should be based on your personal experience.

Try to think of a situation where actions were more important than words. Maybe a friend said they would help you, but let you down. Maybe you know somebody who says they are kind to others, but does not act this way. Focus on describing 2 or 3 examples of how this proverb relates to events that have happened or people you know.

Writing to Explain – Writing Task 3

Read this proverb about change.

A leopard cannot change its spots.

Do you agree with this proverb? Explain why or why not. Use facts, details, or examples in your answer.

Hint

A proverb is a short saying that states an idea. The idea in this proverb is that people cannot change. You have to explain whether or not you agree with this.

When you are asked whether or not you agree with something, you will not be scored based on whether you agree or not. You will be scored on how well you explain why you do or do not agree. Don't worry about choosing the right answer. Instead, focus on what your personal opinion is. Then focus on clearly explaining why this is your opinion.

Writing to Explain – Writing Task 4

Think about your friendships. What do you think makes a good friend? Use facts, details, or examples to support your opinion.

Hint

When completing these writing tasks, it is important to include supporting details. In some tasks, you can use facts. In a task like this, it is often better to use details and examples.

Once you have decided what makes a good friend, thinks of details and examples you can use to support your opinion. For example, imagine that you think that a good friend is always there for you. You could support this idea by describing a situation where you needed a friend and your friend was there for you.

Writing to Explain – Writing Task 5

Read this piece of advice.

Don't put all your eggs in one basket.

Do you think this is good advice? Explain why or why not.

Hint

Start by thinking about what the advice means. It means that you should not rely on just one thing too much. Then think about whether you agree. Think about how this advice relates to your life.

The advice can be applied to many areas. A good essay will be focused. Think about how it relates to one area of your life. It could be your studies, your friendships, or your goals. As you plan your writing, focus on this one area. This will help make sure you produce writing that has a clear and focused idea.

Answer Key

The SOL Reading and Writing tests given by the state assess a specific set of skills. Student learning is based on these standards throughout the year, and the state tests include questions that assess whether students have the skills described in the standards.

Each question in Section 1 of this book assesses one specific skill. The answer key identifies the skill covered by each question. Use the skill listed with each question to identify areas of strength and weakness. Then target revision and instruction accordingly.

Section 1: Revising and Editing Quizzes

Set 1

Quiz 1

Question	Answer	Revising and Editing Skill
1	See Below	Use contractions correctly
2	C	Identify rhyming words
3	D	Combine sentences correctly
4	B	Use correct verbs and correct verb tense
5	B	Use homophones correctly*

*Homophones are words that are pronounced the same but have different meanings, such as the words *ate* and *eight*.

Q1. The student should write the following long form of each contraction:
- it is, could not, I have, will not

Quiz 2

Question	Answer	Revising and Editing Skill
1	See Below	Identify and write words with silent letters
2	B	Use correct punctuation (dates)
3	D	Revise sentences for clarity and correctness
4	B	Use pronouns correctly

Q1. The student should circle the silent letter indicated below. The student should then write two words that have the same silent letter. Sample answers are given below.
- lam**b**: thumb, bomb, dumb, crumb, limb, debt, doubt, climb
- g**h**ost: whale, school, echo, chord, honest, hour, rhino
- **k**nife: knee, knot, knock, know, knew, kneel, knack
- **w**rong: wreck, wrestle, wrinkle, wrist, write, wrap, sword

Quiz 3

Question	Answer	Revising and Editing Skill
1	B	Use correct verbs and correct verb tense
2	B	Combine sentences correctly
3	B	Use correct capitalization
4	A	Spell words correctly
5	D	Identify and use antonyms

Quiz 4

Question	Answer	Revising and Editing Skill
1	See Below	Identify and use adjectives
2	C	Spell words correctly (commonly misspelled words)
3	A	Identify rhyming words
4	C	Use correct verbs and correct verb tense
5	C	Understand and use words with affixes

Q1. The student should complete the sentences as listed below:
- A stingray's fins are <u>large</u> and <u>flat</u>.
- Each fin looks a bit like a wing that is <u>giant</u>.
- The stingray's stingers are <u>pointy</u> and <u>sharp</u>.
- Stingray's hide under a layer of sand that is <u>thin</u>.

Quiz 5

Question	Answer	Revising and Editing Skill
1	See Below	Identify and write compound words
2	C	Combine sentences correctly
3	C	Use irregular verbs correctly
4	D	Use correct punctuation (apostrophes)

Q1. The student should list three compounds words ending with the same end word. Sample answers are given below.
- classroom: bedroom, ballroom, bathroom, showroom, sunroom, legroom
- baseball: basketball, football, fastball, fireball, snowball, softball, eyeball
- daytime: bedtime, nighttime, teatime, playtime, overtime, halftime, lifetime

Set 2

Quiz 6

Question	Answer	Revising and Editing Skill
1	See Below	Use correct punctuation (end punctuation)
2	C	Use correct verbs and correct verb tense
3	B	Edit sentences for clarity and correctness
4	D	Use correct subject-verb agreement
5	D	Use phonics to identify and compare word sounds

Q1.   The student should explain that the exclamation mark is suitable. The student may explain that it helps show how excited Brin felt.

Quiz 7

Question	Answer	Revising and Editing Skill
1	See Below	Spell words correctly (commonly misspelled words)
2	C	Use words with suffixes correctly
3	D	Revise sentences for clarity and correctness
4	D	Revise passages for clarity and relevance
5	A	Identify and use synonyms

Q1.   The student should circle the following correct spellings: people, little, sister, mother, children, and favorite.

Quiz 8

Question	Answer	Revising and Editing Skill
1	See Below	Place words in alphabetical order
2	A	Determine the meaning of words with multiple meanings
3	D	Identify rhyming words
4	B	Revise sentences for clarity and coherence

Q1.   The student should list the names in the order below:
- Feathers, Fergie, Frankie, Fuzzy

Quiz 9

Question	Answer	Revising and Editing Skill
1	See Below	Spell words with suffixes correctly
2	B	Use correct punctuation (end punctuation)
3	B	Understand the use of pronouns
4	C	Use transition words and phrases effectively

Q1. The student should write the following words: stopping, skipping, cutting, running, rubbing.

Quiz 10

Question	Answer	Revising and Editing Skill
1	B	Determine the meaning of words with multiple meanings
2	A	Revise sentences for clarity and coherence
3	B	Use correct punctuation (commas)
4	D	Revise passages for clarity and relevance

Set 3

Quiz 11

Question	Answer	Revising and Editing Skill
1	See Below	Identify and write rhyming words
2	D	Identify different types of words (adjectives)
3	D	Spell words correctly
4	D	Identify compound words
5	A	Use contractions correctly

Q1.   The student should circle the words listed below. The students should then write another rhyming word. Sample answers are given below.

- care, chair: air, bear, wear, stare
- hope, soap: cope, rope, mope, slope
- rain, plain: brain, cane, main, vein
- wart, sort: short, taught, court, port
- night, write: light, height, white, kite

Quiz 12

Question	Answer	Revising and Editing Skill
1	C	Revise passages for organization
2	B	Make connections between passage content and art
3	D	Combine sentences correctly
4	B	Revise sentences for clarity and coherence
5	C	Revise sentences for clarity and correctness

Quiz 13

Question	Answer	Revising and Editing Skill
1	See Below	Use phonics to identify words
2	B	Identify complete and incomplete sentences
3	C	Use correct subject-verb agreement
4	D	Use irregular plurals correctly
5	B	Understand and use homophones*

*Homophones are words that are pronounced the same but have different meanings, such as the words *ate* and *eight*.

Q1.   The student should write the following words: stay, tray, clay, and gray.

Quiz 14

Question	Answer	Revising and Editing Skill
1	See Below	Identify the number of syllables in a word
2	A	Combine sentences correctly
3	B	Revise sentences for clarity and coherence
4	D	Revise sentences for clarity and coherence

Q1. The student should list the words in the table as below:
- One-syllable words: pet, seeds, wings, clean, mess
- Two-syllable words: parrot, enjoys, water, mother, eating

Quiz 15

Question	Answer	Revising and Editing Skill
1	B	Use irregular plurals correctly
2	A	Understand the meaning of prefixes
3	C	Use correct capitalization
4	D	Use transition words effectively
5	C	Revise sentences for clarity and coherence

Set 4

Quiz 16

Question	Answer	Revising and Editing Skill
1	A	Use correct subject-verb agreement
2	B	Identify different types of words (verbs)
3	C	Choose a relevant topic sentence
4	A	Revise sentences for clarity and coherence
5	C	Use correct punctuation (commas)

Quiz 17

Question	Answer	Revising and Editing Skill
1	See Below	Use correct punctuation (dialogue)
2	A	Use correct verbs and correct verb tense
3	D	Edit sentences for correctness
4	C	Combine sentences correctly

Q1.   The student should rewrite the sentences as shown below:
- "Where are you going?" Rachel asked.
- "I am busy right now," Kyra said.

Quiz 18

Question	Answer	Revising and Editing Skill
1	See Below	Identify and write compound words
2	B	Revise passages for organization
3	D	Identify complete and incomplete sentences
4	C	Choose a relevant concluding sentence
5	C	Edit sentences for correctness

Q1.   The student should list three compounds words with the word part shown. Sample answers are given below.
- bookmark, bookend, bookcase, bookshop, bookshelf, bookworm
- doorstop, doorknob, doorman, doorway, doorbell, doormat
- fireman, mailman, snowman, workman, handyman, watchman

Quiz 19

Question	Answer	Revising and Editing Skill
1	See Below	Understand and use homonyms*
2	A	Use correct subject-verb agreement
3	D	Spell words correctly
4	A	Revise sentences for clarity and coherence
5	D	Revise sentences for clarity and correctness

*Homonyms are words that have the same spelling and are pronounced the same, but have different meanings.

Q1. The student should give a meaning of *post* other than "a pole" and a meaning of *feet* other than "a unit of measure." Sample answers are given below.
   • to put something in the mail
   • the part of the body at the end of the leg

Quiz 20

Question	Answer	Revising and Editing Skill
1	See Below	Identify nouns and proper nouns
2	A	Identify and use synonyms
3	B	Spell words with suffixes correctly
4	D	Understand the meaning of suffixes
5	C	Use contractions correctly

Q1. The student should list any three of the nouns and proper nouns below.
   • Nouns: gases, crust, place, spaceship, rocket, scientists, camera, photos, moons
   • Proper nouns: Sun, Solar System, Earth

Section 2: Language, Vocabulary, and Grammar Quizzes

Quiz 21: Analyze Words

1. A
2. C
3. D
4. D

Quiz 22: Write and Spell Words Correctly

1. bear	2. sheep
3. boat	4. goat
5. bread	6. plane
7. clock	8. coin

Quiz 23: Identify Correct Spellings

1. white	5. pear	9. whale
2. blue	6. peach	10. toad
3. green	7. lime	11. seal
4. red	8. grape	12. goose

Quiz 24: Place Words in Alphabetical Order

1. B
2. A
3. B
4. three, tiger, train, twist

Quiz 25: Divide Words into Syllables

1. mon / key	9. el / e / phant
2. be / fore	10. af / ter / noon
3. cir / cus	11. fam / i / ly
4. hap / py	12. tel / e / phone
5. let / ter	13. to / mor / row
6. nev / er	14. won / der / ful
7. win / dow	
8. yel / low	

Quiz 26: Understand and Use Abbreviations

1. Ave.	8. ft
2. Rd.	9. yd
3. St.	10. oz
4. Dr.	11. lb
5. Jr.	12. cm
6. Mr.	
7. Dr.	

Quiz 27: Identify and Use Antonyms

1. B
2. C
3. A
4. C

Quiz 28: Identify Base Words

1. B
2. D
3. B
4. B

Quiz 29: Use Plurals Correctly

1. picnic	6. bikes
2. windows	7. clock
3. street	8. leaves
4. room	9. mouse
5. bottles	10. lives

Quiz 30: Identify Proper Nouns

1. Sunday
2. June
3. Sarah
4. Florida
5. Canada
6. Walmart

Quiz 31: Use Words with Suffixes

1. B
2. A
3. C
4. A

Quiz 32: Spell Commonly Misspelled Words

1. favorite
2. friends
3. always
4. said
5. people
6. scared

Quiz 33: Understand and Use Prefixes

1. B
2. A
3. B
4. D

Quiz 34: Understand and Use Suffixes

1. B
2. C
3. B
4. B

Quiz 35: Spell Words with Suffixes Correctly

1. C
2. C
3. A
4. C

Quiz 36: Use Contractions

Sentences will vary. Any sentence that uses the contraction correctly is acceptable.

1. you're
2. he'll
3. that's
4. isn't
5. you've
6. didn't

Quiz 37: Identify and Use Synonyms

1. B
2. B
3. C
4. B

Quiz 38: Identify Types of Words
1. ran, quickly
2. won, close
3. baked, beautiful
4. washed, dirty
5. bought, large
6. looked, green

Quiz 39: Use Correct Verb Tense
1. D
2. B
3. B
4. A

Quiz 40: Use Pronouns
1. D
2. A
3. B
4. C

Quiz 41: Use Words to Show Time Order
1. C
2. A
3. B
4. D

Quiz 42: Understand Word Meanings
1. B
2. B
3. C

Quiz 43: Spell Words Correctly
1. D
2. D
3. C
4. B

Quiz 44: Use Correct Punctuation
1. B
2. B
3. C
4. ? / ! / .

Quiz 45: Identify Base Words and Suffixes

1. drive / ing
2. talk / ed
3. stop / ed
4. pull / ing
5. make / s
6. smile / ed

Quiz 46: Use Homophones

1. B
2. B
3. C
4. D

Quiz 47: Use Homographs

Answers will vary. Sample answers are given below.

1. I hit the ball with a bat. / The bat flew out of the cave.
2. I played in the park. / My mother tried to park the car.
3. It is fun to dance to rock music. / I threw a rock into the lake.
4. The big ocean wave knocked me over. / It is nice to wave to people you know.
5. The light outside was bright. / The feather was very light.

Quiz 48: Use Correct Subject-Verb Agreement

1. A
2. B
3. D
4. D

Section 3: Guided Writing Tasks

Writing to Entertain

Score each writing task by giving the student a score out of 5 for each of the four criteria. Add the scores to give a final score out of 20. After scoring the writing task, review with students areas where they have scored well and areas where the scores could be improved. Give students guidance on what to focus on in the next writing task to improve their score.

	Task 1	Task 2	Task 3	Task 4	Task 5
Content and Organization To receive a full score, the response will: • have a beginning, middle, and end • have a clear focus • have well-developed ideas • have good transitions between ideas • be clear and easy to understand					
Word Usage To receive a full score, the response will: • use correct verb tense • have correct subject-verb agreement • use pronouns correctly • use words with the correct meaning • use a variety of words • show evidence of well-chosen words					
Sentence Construction To receive a full score, the response will: • use a variety of sentence structures • construct sentences correctly					
Mechanics To receive a full score, the response will: • have few or no spelling errors • have few or no capitalization errors • have few or no punctuation errors					
Total Score					

Writing to Describe

Score each writing task by giving the student a score out of 5 for each of the four criteria. Add the scores to give a final score out of 20. After scoring the writing task, review with students areas where they have scored well and areas where the scores could be improved. Give students guidance on what to focus on in the next writing task to improve their score.

	Task 1	Task 2	Task 3	Task 4	Task 5
Content and Organization To receive a full score, the response will: • have an opening and a closing • be focused • have well-developed ideas • have good transitions between ideas • be clear and easy to understand					
Word Usage To receive a full score, the response will: • use correct verb tense • have correct subject-verb agreement • use pronouns correctly • use words with the correct meaning					
Sentence Construction To receive a full score, the response will: • use a variety of sentence structures • construct sentences correctly					
Mechanics To receive a full score, the response will: • have few or no spelling errors • have few or no capitalization errors • have few or no punctuation errors					
Total Score					

Writing to Explain

Score each writing task by giving the student a score out of 5 for each of the four criteria. Add the scores to give a final score out of 20. After scoring the writing task, review with students areas where they have scored well and areas where the scores could be improved. Give students guidance on what to focus on in the next writing task to improve their score.

	Task 1	Task 2	Task 3	Task 4	Task 5
Content and Organization To receive a full score, the response will: • have an opening and a closing • have a clear focus • have well-developed ideas • have good transitions between ideas • be clear and easy to understand • use supporting details					
Word Usage To receive a full score, the response will: • use correct verb tense • have correct subject-verb agreement • use pronouns correctly • use words with the correct meaning					
Sentence Construction To receive a full score, the response will: • use a variety of sentence structures • construct sentences correctly					
Mechanics To receive a full score, the response will: • have few or no spelling errors • have few or no capitalization errors • have few or no punctuation errors					
Total Score					

Virginia Test Prep Practice Test Book

For additional reading test prep, get the Virginia Test Prep Practice Test Book. It contains 6 reading mini-tests, focused vocabulary quizzes, plus a full-length SOL Reading practice test.

Made in the USA
Lexington, KY
07 March 2014